D0572402

BUSY BAGS
♥ KIDS WILL LOVE ♥

MAKE-AHEAD ACTIVITY KITS FOR A HAPPY PRESCHOOLER AND STRESS-FREE PARENT

★ SARA McCLURE ★

Ulysses Press

Text and photographs copyright © 2017 Sara McClure. Design and concept copyright © 2017 Ulysses Press and its licensors. All rights reserved. Any unauthorized duplication in whole or in part or dissemination of this edition by any means (including but not limited to photocopying, electronic devices, digital versions, and the Internet) will be prosecuted to the fullest extent of the law.

Published in the U.S. by
Ulysses Press
P.O. Box 3440
Berkeley, CA 94703
www.ulyssespress.com

ISBN: 978-1-61243-667-8
Library of Congress Control Number 20169567510

Printed in Korea by WE SP through Four Colour Print Group

10 9 8 7 6 5 4 3 2 1

Acquisitions editor: Bridget Thoreson
Managing editor: Claire Chun
Editor: Shayna Keyles
Proofreader: Lauren Harrison
Cover design: Michelle Thompson
Interior design and layout: what!design @ whatweb.com

Distributed by Publishers Group West

TABLE OF CONTENTS

PREFACE 5

INTRODUCTION 6

What Are Busy Bags? 6

Why Should You Use Busy Bags? 6

Who Can Use Busy Bags? 7

How Are Busy Bags Stored? 7

Hosting a Busy Bag Swap 7

100 Things Kids Should Know Before Entering Kindergarten 8

PART 1: MATH 11

STICKER CLIP CARDS 14

SHAPE BUILDERS 17

GEOBOARD SHAPES 19

THREE BEARS SIZE SORT 21

FISHING FOR NUMBERS 23

PAPER CLIP COLOR SORT 26

KITE BOW COUNTING 28

POPSICLE STICK PATTERNS 31

DECK OF CARDS MIX-UP 33

MEDICINE BOX COLOR MATCH 35

POM-POM NUMBER CATERPILLARS 36

POPSICLE STICK NUMBER CLIP 38

EGG CARTON COLOR MATCH 40

SPOON NUMBER MATCH 42

COUNTING CATERPILLAR 44

RAINBOW STICK 46

BLOCK SHADOWS 48

PART 2: LITERACY 50

BUILD A WORD 52

NAME PUZZLES 54

SPAGHETTI SPELLING 56

FISHING FOR LETTERS 57

SPOON ABC MATCH 60

ABC STICKER PUZZLES 62

I SPY LETTERS! 64

PART 3: FINE MOTOR SKILLS 66

BUTTON SNAKE 70

SILLY STRAW THREADING 72

NUTS AND BOLTS 74

SHOE TYING PRACTICE BOARD 75

ZIPPER BOARD 77

LACING SHAPES 79

PIPE CLEANER POKE 81

PUT IT IN YOUR WALLET 82

PHOTO BOOK TRACING 84

BUTTON TURKEY 86

BUTTON FLOWERS 88

POKER CHIP PUSH 90

FELT BUTTON CHAIN 92

PART 4: JUST FOR FUN 94

MATCHING GAME 96

SOCK FISHING GAME 98

COOKIE CUTTER MATCH-UP 101

BUILD A FACE 103

BUILD AN OCEAN 105

BUILD A MONSTER 107

BUILD A ROBOT 109

BUILD A JACK-O-LANTERN 111

BUILD A GINGERBREAD MAN 113

BUILD A SNOWMAN 115

PEG DOLL DRESS UP 117

JEWELRY BOX MATCH-UP 119

POPSICLE STICK PICTURE PUZZLES 121

POPSICLE STICK HIGHWAY 123

RICE SENSORY BIN 125

ACKNOWLEDGMENTS 128

ABOUT THE AUTHOR 128

PREFACE

When my two boys were younger, it seemed like they were interested in everything. They always needed to be busy. I found that parenting and running a household with all of its demands was hard work with little ones around. I needed things to keep my children busy for short amounts of time just so I could make dinner or clean the bathroom without "helpers." I often had them at the table coloring, putting together puzzles, or playing with little activities to keep them out of the way while I accomplished my long to-do list.

When I started homeschooling my oldest, I struggled to keep my mischievous toddler entertained while I taught. Every time I turned around, he was dumping the toy baskets, making messes, and getting himself into trouble. That's when I started making and using busy bags.

At first, these busy bags were a super simple way to keep my toddler's little hands busy for a few moments in the highchair while I taught his brother math. As he grew, the bags became more complex to keep his attention for longer. Busy bags saved my sanity when I needed it most. Even today, I still use busy bags to help him practice preschool skills. They double as part of his preschool curriculum and I still have a few moments to teach math to my oldest.

Maybe you're like me and find yourself stressed out with little ones underfoot. Maybe you, too, need to keep the kids busy while you make dinner or clean the bathroom. Busy bags can help relieve that stress. Inside this book, you'll find 52 ways to keep your little one busy. With one activity a week, you'll have an entire year's worth of fun in this book that was written with your little one in mind.

It is my hope that this book helps take the stress out of your life when it comes to keeping your child occupied. I've used my knowledge as a certified teacher to make sure these activities are learning based and developmentally appropriate. I've taken the guesswork out of it, so you can get straight to the good stuff. There will be no need to search the Internet for hours trying to find something to make—it's all here.

Please note that this book is intended as a way to enhance a child's learning environment. You know your child best and how he interacts with materials; please observe caution and safety at all times. All activities should be used with adult supervision. Appropriate caution should be used when activities call for materials that could present a choking risk.

Are you ready to get to work? Good. Three cheers for stress-free parenting!

INTRODUCTION

WHAT ARE BUSY BAGS?

Busy bags are activities for children to play with that have been made ahead of time. Sometimes called quiet bins or quiet boxes, busy bags can be a saving grace to a parent that needs to keep a young child occupied for a short amount of time. Gone are the days of letting the kids play in the cabinets at your feet while you cook dinner. Busy bags are emerging as the answer for stressed-out, busy parents. These activities can help take you from stressed out to stress-free.

Items in busy bags can range from those meant for educational concepts to things placed there just for fun. There really are no set rules for what goes into a busy bag. If you think your child will play with it for an extended amount of time, it's fair game. Learning through play is best for children, so it stands to reason that the play-oriented busy bags are teaching kids just as much as the ones intended for educational purposes only.

Busy bags are self-contained, almost like a kit of activities. Busy bags take a little effort to make on the front end, but once they are made, you will have an arsenal of activities that can be used at a moment's notice. Preparing busy bags is definitely worth it!

WHY SHOULD YOU USE BUSY BAGS?

Busy bags, to put it simply, keep your kids busy! Whether it's while you cook dinner or during quiet time, busy bags can help keep your little ones occupied while you accomplish simple household tasks. I've known parents to use busy bags while they clean, cook, or help an older child with homework. Others may use busy bags to keep the little ones busy while homeschooling older children. Then there are the parents who use busy bags as pre-planned activities to connect with their child whenever they have a few minutes of free time.

Most busy bags are portable, so they are easy to take to a doctor's office waiting room or even out to a restaurant to keep a child occupied while waiting on your food. Often, those places are filled with angst and frustration while you wait with a fussy toddler or preschooler. Busy bags can be the answer in those important waiting times.

WHO CAN USE BUSY BAGS?

Busy bags aren't just for parents. Caregivers, babysitters, and even teachers are using busy bags to engage little learners in meaningful play activities.

HOW ARE BUSY BAGS STORED?

Busy bags can be stored in a variety of ways—in simple plastic gallon-size storage bags, bins, or boxes. Depending on the size of the activity, busy bag games can also be stored in a pencil pouch. I've even seen tiny activities placed in a small, recycled mints container. Basically, anything goes!

Storage for the pre-made kits can vary as well. Some choose to store them in a basket or in tote boxes, keeping them accessible to the kids at all times. Others like to store their busy bags on hooks in the playroom. Some people rotate the activities weekly to keep their child's interest. How you store and when you choose to use your busy bags are ultimately up to you and what works for your environment.

HOSTING A BUSY BAG SWAP

Wouldn't it be great to get an assortment of busy bags in less time than it takes to make them all? One popular way to get an assortment of busy bags at once is to host a busy bag swap. That way, you can avoid the stress of finding, purchasing, and making all the materials for each busy bag.

The basic idea of a busy bag swap is for each person in the group to pick one busy bag to make. Everyone will assemble an identical busy bag for each person in the group. At the swap time, each member will bring their completed busy bags and swaps with all the participants. In the end, each person will go home with several different busy bags. It's a win-win situation for everyone involved. So grab a group of friends, and get swapping!

Some things to consider when hosting a busy bag swap:

- Set a limit on the number of participants. Ten participants is a good number, but there is no rule here. Just remember: the more participants, the more bags you have to make.
- Set a price limit to keep costs down. I think a good number is $1.00 per bag. For some busy bags, you can get by with spending much less depending on the materials, but it is good to set a price limit for all the participants to stick to and keep costs down.

- Acknowledge the time it takes to make the busy bags. Allow at least three or four weeks for all participants to make their busy bags. Some people may be able to knock their busy bags out in one afternoon, but others might need more time to make everything.

- Pick a place to exchange the bags. It is easiest to host at someone's house where you can spread the bags out. Then, everyone can go down the line to grab their new busy bags.

- At the busy bag swap, take time for each person to explain how to play with the busy bag. It's easier if the instructions are included in the bag, too.

- Think about how the busy bags will be stored. It's easiest to have everyone place their busy bag activities in gallon-size plastic bags. This keeps things consistent and easier to manage.

- Make sure everyone knows what they are making ahead of time so there aren't any duplicates.

100 THINGS KIDS SHOULD KNOW BEFORE ENTERING KINDERGARTEN

Preparing children for success in school is one of the top priorities of parents. Knowing the expectations for your child can help you support the development of the skills needed to start school. Listed below are 100 common skills that will help set your child up for success. It is important to note that children can develop at different rates, but the goals remain the same for all. Use this list as a guide for preparing your child for kindergarten, but don't stress if they don't complete all of these goals before they start school. Help your child learn to:

1. Manage bathroom needs
2. Wash hands after using the bathroom
3. Wipe nose with a tissue
4. Button shirt, coat, and pants
5. Zip up zippers
6. Try to tie own shoes
7. Put on a coat
8. Put on a backpack
9. Open a juice box and a small carton of milk
10. Carry a plate of food without spilling
11. Drink from a water fountain
12. Separate from parents without being upset
13. Know first and last name
14. Know address
15. Know phone number
16. Show eagerness and curiosity as a learner
17. Persist in tasks, and seek help when encountering a problem
18. Stay with an activity to completion
19. Be generally pleasant and cooperative
20. Use phrases like "please," "thank you," and "excuse me"

21. Follow rules and routines

22. Manage transitions between one activity and the next

23. Complete activities and tasks at normal speed (not too fast, not too slow)

24. Interact easily with one or more children

25. Interact easily with familiar adults

26. Participate in group activities

27. Play well with others

28. Take turns and share

29. Clean up after play

30. Seek adult help when it is needed to resolve conflicts

31. Use words to resolve conflicts

32. Understand actions have both causes and effects

33. Listen and understand directions and conversations

34. Follow one-step directions

35. Follow two-step directions

36. Pay attention to adult-directed tasks for short periods of time

37. Speak clearly enough to be understood without contextual clues

38. Have some understanding of sequences of events

39. Listen with interest to stories read aloud, without interrupting

40. Show interest in reading-related activities

41. Retell information from a story

42. Sequence three pictures to tell a logical story

43. Know and recite some common nursery rhymes and songs

44. Repeat a six- to eight-word sentence

45. Recognize rhyming sounds

46. Use pictures to communicate ideas

47. Use scribbles, shapes, and letter-like symbols to write words or ideas

48. Hold a book and turn pages

49. Understand how to track words from left to right

50. Understand what side of a book is the front and what page comes first

51. Recite or sing the alphabet

52. Match uppercase letters to uppercase letters

53. Match lowercase letters to lowercase letters

54. Identify uppercase and lowercase letters and match them accordingly

55. Identify some letter sounds

56. Identify the beginning sound of some words

57. Sort by color, shape, and size

58. Order, or seriate, several objects based on a single linking attribute

59. Recognize and duplicate simple patterns

60. Count to 20

61. Use finger to touch-count up to 10 items

62. Match numerals to a corresponding number of objects

63. Identify numerals 0 through 10 in random order

64. Identify what number comes before or after a given number, up to 10

65. Identify circle, square, rectangle, and triangle

66. Demonstrate concepts of positional and directional concepts, like up/down and over/under

67. Show understanding of and use comparative words, like big/little and short/long

68. Pedal and steer a tricycle

69. Jump in place, landing on two feet

70. Jump seven consecutive jumps

71. Balance on one foot for five seconds

72. Hop on one foot for two to three hops, then switch and repeat on the opposite foot

73. Hop on one foot for 6 feet

74. Throw a ball with direction up to 5 feet

75. Catch a thrown ball with arms and body

76. Bounce a ball

77. Climb a playground ladder

78. Skip smoothly for 20 feet

79. Show understanding of general times of day

80. Stack ten 1-inch blocks

81. String four ½-inch beads in two minutes

82. Complete a seven-piece interlocking puzzle

83. Make a pancake, snake, and ball from Play-Doh

84. Grasp pencil correctly

85. Copy a vertical line, horizontal line, circle, cross, square, V, and triangle

86. Copy first name

87. Print first name without a model

88. Grasp scissors correctly

89. Cut within ¼ inch of a 6-inch straight line on construction paper

90. Cut out a 3-inch square on construction paper

91. Cut out a 3-inch triangle on construction paper

92. Cut out a 3-inch circle on construction paper

93. Use a glue stick appropriately

94. Use an appropriate amount of glue for tasks

95. Identify 10 colors: red, yellow, blue, green, orange, purple, black, white, brown, and pink

96. Use a variety of art materials for tactile experience and exploration

97. Participate in group music experiences

98. Participate in creative movement and dance

99. Make believe with objects

100. Take on pretend roles and situations

The activities in this book were designed with this list in mind. It is my hope that the busy bags support you and your child for kindergarten preparation.

PART 1: MATH

MATH DEVELOPMENT IN THE EARLY YEARS

Most people, when asked about early math development, will tell you that young children need to learn counting and numbers. While this is true, there are many other areas in math development for little learners to focus on. With the current education standards and the pressure placed on schools to teach math (and teach it well), the pressure trickles down to the youngest of learners. Kindergarten students are being asked to do more and more when kindergarten used to be about play. Sound overwhelming? It's a tall order, for sure.

Early math is not about rotely learning arithmetic equations like 1+1=2, or even about completing worksheets where there is only one correct answer for any given problem. Early math development should be playful and encourage children to make sense of the world around them. Playful math exploration encourages children to solve problems in real-life situations. For example, it is easier for children to understand what the number 2 means when they are stringing two beads on a string, or passing out two cookies to friends.

Preschoolers naturally explore and experiment with math concepts. They might talk about being taller than a friend, which uses measurement. Or they might naturally sort their toys into categories. As parents and teachers, we must engage that exploration of math in our little learners.

Even for young learners, math is more than a numbers game. There are many dimensions to early math, including:

- Number sense
- Geometry
- Measurement
- The language of math
- Spatial relations

Number sense is when children know the number "5" represents five objects. It is also when children know that five is less than six, but more than four. Counting also falls under this category. Develop this skill with young children by counting snacks at snack time, using a calendar to count down the days to an important event, and playing board games where the child has to move a game piece a certain number of spaces.

Geometry in a child's early years involves learning the shapes and knowing they have unique features. For example, a triangle has three sides, but a square has four. Early geometry also includes learning to make patterns. Develop this skill with young children by having them name shapes of objects, pointing out the corners and sides of objects, and making patterns with snacks (for example: raisin, cracker, raisin, cracker…).

Measurement concepts for young children include size, distance, and amounts. Young children often compare their heights with their friends' or compare their ages to their siblings'. Anyone that has given snacks to multiple children knows that they have a strong knowledge of when someone else has more than they do. Develop this skill in young children by helping them measure ingredients for a recipe or by measuring their height with a growth chart and comparing how much they have grown.

The language of math in the early years sounds like "more," "less," and "same." These terms then change to "more than," "less than," and "equal to" as children gain more knowledge in math and go to school. Develop this skill in young children by discussing and helping them understand concepts like more than and less than, bigger and smaller, and so on.

Spatial relations is when children understand when objects are behind or in front of each other, or when something is near or far. Develop this skill in young children by playing games where they have to jump forward and backward, and by using songs with corresponding movements to teach in and out, up and down, and round and round.

If you watch young children, you'll be surprised at how often they use these concepts in any given day through words and actions.

MATH BUSY BAGS

The activities in this section are designed to address these early math concepts. Each activity will have target skills listed. Some of the terms you will see are one-to-one correspondence, counting, number sense, number identification, sorting, and patterns. These mathematical skills are the foundation of early math learning. To make sure you understand these terms and their importance, I want to highlight a few key ideas for these skills.

One-to-One Correspondence

Rote counting involves memorizing the number words in the proper order (one, two, three, four, five…). Young children are also capable of recognizing numbers from one to ten. They can learn the number names and recognize the number symbols. However, the ordered numbers often become like a song with no meaning behind them.

One-to-one correspondence is the ability to use the knowledge of number names and shapes to skillfully count actual objects. A child that understands one-to-one correspondence knows that two cookies equals "two," or that five raisins equals "five."

Many young children have memorized the number words in the proper order, but sometimes they do not yet understand the concept of one-to-one correspondence. For example, when counting objects, a child might say "one, two, three, four, five," but skip an object, or they might count an object twice. Children need many opportunities to practice matching one number with one object. One way to practice this skill is to have the child touch each object, or touch-count, when counting.

Sorting

Sorting is a foundational skill in math. By sorting, children will understand that things can be organized into certain groups based on whether they are alike or different. Getting practice with sorting at an early age is important for learning numerical concepts and grouping numbers and sets when they are older. This type of thinking starts them on the path of applying logical thinking to objects, mathematical concepts, and everyday life. There are many ways to sort objects. In the activities in this section, we will focus on sorting by color and by size.

Patterns

Patterns are all around us. Patterns can be found in words, symbols, numbers, and images. They can also be found in behavior, routines, and in nature. By understanding patterns, children are able to make predictions about what should come next. Children naturally encounter patterns during the day. A perfect example of this is a bedtime routine. Children know the order in which they usually put their pajamas on, brush their teeth, read stories, and go to bed every single night. Or they might have a pattern on their clothing, like a striped shirt. Teaching children how to make and extend patterns sets them up for skip counting (or counting by multiples) and multiplication in the later years.

The following math busy bags are fun and play-based because that's how young children learn best. Yes, learning can and should be fun!

STICKER CLIP CARDS

There's no doubt about it—kids love stickers. Channel your inner kid to make these easy number identification cards with a fine-motor twist.

TARGET SKILLS: counting, number identification, number sense, one-to-one correspondence, fine motor skills

MATERIALS

- cardstock, or thin cardboard from a recycled cereal box
- scissors
- ruler
- marker
- small stickers
- laminator (optional)
- clothespins

DIRECTIONS TO MAKE

1. Cut the cardstock into 4 pieces. Or, if you are using thin cardboard from cereal boxes, cut rectangles that are approximately 4½ × 5½ inches.

2. Using the ruler, draw a horizontal line on the lower third of the rectangle cardstock pieces. Then, underneath the horizontal line, draw two vertical lines an equal distance apart to create three rectangles of the same size.

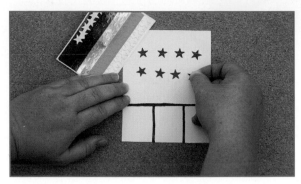

3. Place the stickers on the top portion of the cardstock or thin cardboard. On the first card, place one sticker. On the second card, place two stickers. On the third card, place three stickers. Keep doing this until you get to a card with 10 stickers. If you have an older preschooler, go up to 20.

4. Write numbers in the three boxes—one number corresponding to the number of stickers and two random numbers. Laminate for durability, if you'd like.

DIRECTIONS TO PLAY

The child will count the number of stickers on each card. Then, he or she will clip the clothespin onto the correct number on the card.

TIP: To make this a self-checking activity, place a sticker on the back of the card where the clothespin should be when the child chooses the correct answer. When children turn over the card, they will be able to see if they counted correctly.

SHAPE BUILDERS

Shapes are all around us! This shape building activity is perfect for teaching how many sides a square has or for building familiar shapes. As children branch out into making other shapes and sculptures, they are being creative little engineers. This is a perfect STEM (science, technology, engineering, math) activity and encourages mathematical thinking.

TARGET SKILLS: identifying shapes, engineering, hand-eye coordination, fine motor skills

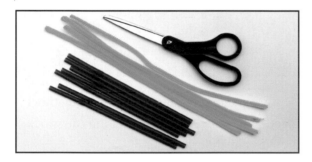

MATERIALS

- 20 straws
- scissors
- 5 pipe cleaners
- 3 pieces of cardstock
- marker
- laminator (optional)

DIRECTIONS TO MAKE

1. If your straws have flexible bends in them, cut this portion off. Then, cut the straws in half, and cut some of those in half again. This will give you various straw lengths.

2. Cut the pipe cleaners in half. Then, cut them in half again.

3. Bend the pipe cleaners into right angles.

4. Cut the cardstock in half.

5. Draw the following shapes on the cardstock: square, triangle, rectangle, pentagon, hexagon, and octagon.

6. Laminate the cardstock for durability, if you'd like.

DIRECTIONS TO PLAY

1. Have the child place a pipe cleaner into a straw opening.

2. Next, place another straw on the other side of the same pipe cleaner.

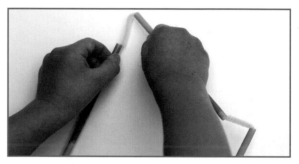

3. Keep placing the pipe cleaners and straws together to make shapes, using the cardstock drawings for reference.

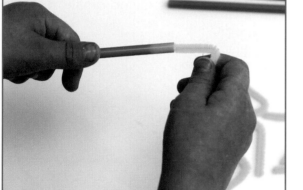

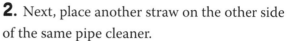

TIP: For further fun, encourage the child to make three-dimensional shapes like cubes or other sculptures. You never know where children's imaginations will take them.

GEOBOARD SHAPES

Children love to play with geoboards to create shapes! Harness this inner motivation to create a fun, open-ended activity. This activity works on shape recognition, building shapes, and the beginning steps to geometry. Also, stretching the rubber bands around the nail pegs is great fine motor work and strengthens hand muscles.

TARGET SKILLS: identifying shapes, fine motor skills

MATERIALS

- ruler
- pencil
- 6 × 6-inch square wood plaque
- hammer
- 1-inch nails
- spray paint (optional)
- scissors
- cardstock
- laminator (optional)
- rubber bands

DIRECTIONS TO MAKE

1. Using the ruler and a pencil, make a grid on the wood plaque. For ours, I made a grid by measuring a ½ inch in from each edge, drawing a 5 × 5-inch square, then marking every inch within the square.

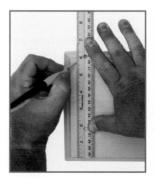 

2. Hammer the nails into the wood plaque at the points of intersection, leaving approximately half an inch of each nail exposed. It is easiest to start on a corner and hammer down the row.

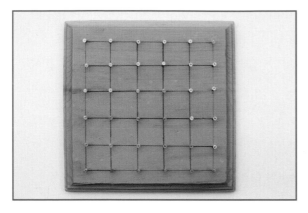

DIRECTIONS TO PLAY

Encourage children to use the rubber bands to make shapes on the geoboard using the cardstock cards for reference, or just let them explore making shapes on their own.

TIP: To help you hammer all of the nails into the board evenly, use a pair of pliers to hold the nail, and hammer in the same amount each time.

3. If you want to spray paint the geoboard, you can.

4. Cut the cardstock into 4 pieces.

5. Draw simple shapes on the cardstock pieces using a marker. For example, you can draw a square, rectangle, triangle, hexagon, octagon, boat, house, fish, and so on. If you'd like, laminate the cardstock pieces for durability.

THREE BEARS SIZE SORT

Use the story Goldilocks and the Three Bears to help little learners practice sorting objects by size. Who will get the biggest objects? Papa Bear! Who will get the medium-sized objects? Mama Bear! Who will get the smallest objects? Baby Bear, of course!

TARGET SKILLS: sorting objects by size

MATERIALS

- 4 pieces of brown cardstock
- pencil or marker
- small plate, bowl, cup, or other small round objects for tracing
- scissors
- glue
- laminator (optional)
- various small, medium, and large objects

DIRECTIONS TO MAKE

1. Using the brown cardstock, make three circles—small, medium, and large. These are going to be the heads of the three bears. Tracing a small plate, a bowl, and a cup will help make the circles. Cut these circles out.

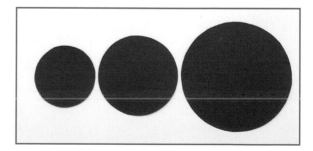

2. Using the brown cardstock, make six smaller circles for the ears. Once again, tracing small round objects, like bottles or jars with different-sized openings, will help make perfect circles. Cut these circles out.

3. Glue the ear pieces to the head circles.

4. Draw a bear face on each bear head. Laminate for durability, if you'd like.

5. Gather various objects that come in small, medium, and large sizes. Try books, paper clips, toy cars, pom-poms, straws cut to size, or envelopes.

6. If you don't have multiple items in three sizes, use your computer and clip art to make different-sized items to sort. Print on card-stock and laminate for durability, if you'd like.

DIRECTIONS TO PLAY

Children will sort the objects by size—small, medium, and large. I like to tell them to pretend the items are for the three bears.

FISHING FOR NUMBERS

Splash! Did you hear that fish? Children will go fishing for numbers in this busy bag. As children complete this activity, they are building number sense and learning numerical order. Practicing identifying the numbers by saying the number out loud helps them to reinforce their number knowledge. By placing the numbers in numerical order, children are learning the basics of a number line and practicing counting in order.

TARGET SKILLS: number identification, counting in order, hand-eye coordination

MATERIALS

- 14 pieces of felt in various colors
- scissors
- template (optional)
- squeezable paint with a writing tip
- hot glue gun
- 20 magnets
- ½-inch × 12-inch dowel rod
- drill
- ¹¹⁄₆₄-inch drill bit
- ⁹⁄₆₄-inch venetian blind cord or other thin cord
- large washer

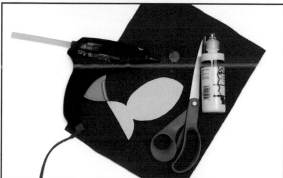

DIRECTIONS TO MAKE

1. Cut 40 identical fish shapes out of the felt. To make this easier, use a copy of the template on page 25 and trace it on the felt before cutting.

2. Using the paint, write the numbers 1 through 20 on 20 fish. Let dry.

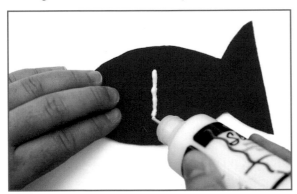

3. Hot glue two fish shapes together, one with a number and one without, placing a magnet inside the mouth area before sealing completely.

4. Measure a ½ inch from the end of the dowel rod. Mark this spot with a pencil.

5. Drill a hole in the dowel rod at the place you marked.

6. Cut the cord to be 24 inches long.

7. Thread the cord through the hole and knot it. To keep the cord from moving too much, tie another knot on the other side close to the dowel rod. There will be cord left hanging.

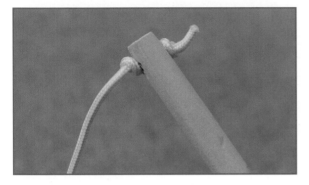

8. Tie the washer to the hanging end of the cord and double knot it.

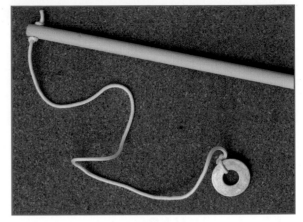

DIRECTIONS TO PLAY

1. Spread the fish on the floor.

2. Children will go fishing for numbers and say the number as they pick up a fish with the fishing pole.

3. If they are older preschoolers, have them start at number 1 and work their way to 20. As they pick up a fish with their fishing pole, have them place the fish in a line. This is an introductory activity to learning a number line.

TEMPLATE FOR FISH

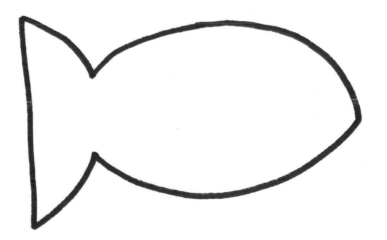

PAPER CLIP COLOR SORT

Kids love to use things usually reserved for grown-ups, so office supplies double as a learning activity in this busy bag. Children will work on sorting by color and strengthening fine motor skills with this activity. As children are sorting by color, they are practicing placing things in groups, a foundational skill in early math. At the same time, they are practicing fine motor skills by placing the paper clips on the paper strip. Kids will flip over using these paper clips!

TARGET SKILLS: sorting objects by color, fine motor skills

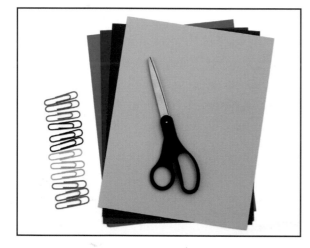

MATERIALS

- colored paper clips (10 of each color; minimum of 4 colors)
- 1 piece of colored cardstock that matches each of the paper clip colors
- scissors
- laminator (optional)

DIRECTIONS TO MAKE

1. Orient your cardstock vertically.

2. Fold the paper in half from left to right.

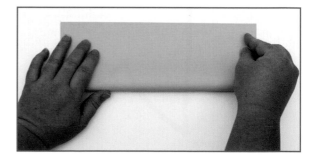

3. Cut the colored cardstock along the fold.

4. Laminate for durability, if you'd like.

DIRECTIONS TO PLAY

Children will sort the paper clips by color and place them on the paper strip with a matching color.

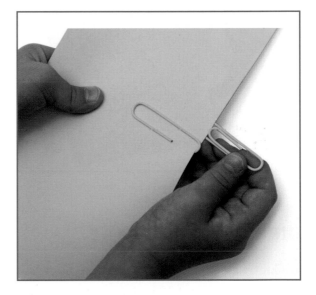

KITE BOW COUNTING

Children's counting skills will soar with this fun kite activity. Children will identify numbers and place the correct number of bows on the kite string. As children count the bows, they are working on one-to-one correspondence.

TARGET SKILLS: counting, number identification, one-to-one correspondence

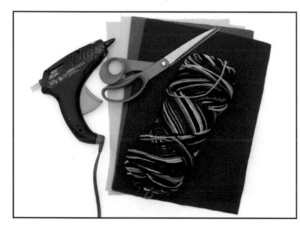

MATERIALS

- 2 pieces of yellow felt
- 1 piece of pink felt
- 3 pieces of purple felt
- template (optional)
- scissors
- yarn
- hot glue gun
- index cards
- marker
- laminator (optional)

DIRECTIONS TO MAKE

1. Cut two identical diamond shapes out of the yellow felt about 12 inches long. This will be the kite.

2. Cut strips of pink felt to make the cross lines on the kite.

3. Cut yarn to be 50 inches long.

4. Hot glue the two diamond pieces together, leaving a small section at the bottom open for the yarn.

5. Place 2 inches of the yarn in the opening and hot glue the rest of the way around the kite.

6. Hot glue the strips of pink felt in a cross pattern on top of the kite.

7. Trim any excess felt away from the strips.

8. Cut 20 bow shapes out of the purple felt. Use the template on page 30.

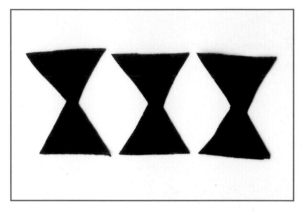

9. On the index cards, write numbers. For younger children, write numbers 1 through 10. For older children, write numbers 1 through 20. Laminate for durability, if you'd like.

DIRECTIONS TO PLAY

1. Children will pick a number card, say the number, and then place the correct number of bows on the string.

2. Once they have completed that number, they will repeat with a new number card.

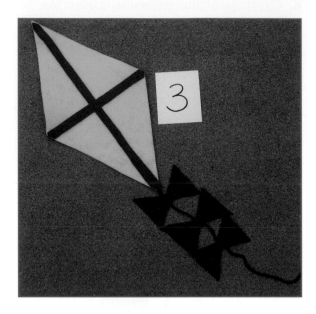

TEMPLATE FOR BOW

POPSICLE STICK PATTERNS

Red, blue, red, blue. I can make a pattern, how about you? Children will make patterns from this busy bag. Making patterns is an important skill in early math development because it sets the foundation for skip counting, addition, and multiplication.

TARGET SKILLS: following patterns, extending patterns

MATERIALS

- 10 jumbo wooden craft sticks
- dot stickers in varying colors
- 1 pack of pom-poms to match the color of the dot stickers
- colored markers (optional)

DIRECTIONS TO MAKE

Place the dot stickers on the jumbo craft sticks in different patterns. For younger preschoolers, use just two alternating colors. For older preschoolers, use more colors and make patterns that are more difficult.

DIRECTIONS TO PLAY

1. Children will place the matching pom-poms on the dot stickers.

2. Older preschoolers can extend the pattern past the craft stick, following the same pattern.

TIP: If you can't find dot stickers to match your pom-poms, use white dot stickers and color them with a marker.

DECK OF CARDS MIX-UP

Who says a deck of cards should be used only for games? Use this busy bag as a matching activity to challenge children to look for matching numbers and suits. Can they find all the clubs, spades, hearts, and diamonds and match them up with the numbers?

TARGET SKILLS: number identification, visual discrimination

MATERIALS

- 1 deck of cards
- scissors

DIRECTIONS TO MAKE

Cut the cards in half. Use various cuts, like curves and zig zags.

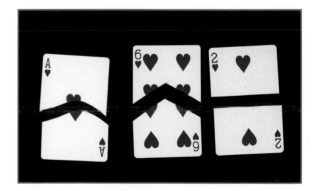

DIRECTIONS TO PLAY

Children will match up the cards.

TIP: If your child is younger, consider only using the cards in one suit instead of the entire deck of cards. For example, only use the numbers with spades on them. As children grow, add more suits to the busy bag.

MEDICINE BOX COLOR MATCH

Let's turn an ordinary and unexpected item into a fun color matching activity! Children will match colors in this busy bag. As they open and close the compartments of the medicine box, they'll be working on fine motor skills, too.

TARGET SKILLS: matching colors, fine motor skills

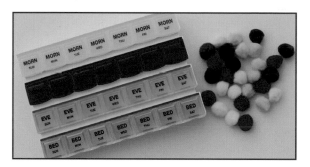

MATERIALS

- large medicine sorting box with colors for each of the days
- colored pom-poms to match the colors on the medicine box
- dot stickers in varying colors (optional)
- colored markers (optional)

DIRECTIONS TO MAKE

1. If you can't find a medicine-sorting box with colored compartments, use colored dot stickers on each compartment to match the colors of your pom-poms.

2. Place the dot stickers, if using, on top of each compartment of the medicine-sorting box.

DIRECTIONS TO PLAY

Children will sort the pom-poms into the corresponding colored compartment.

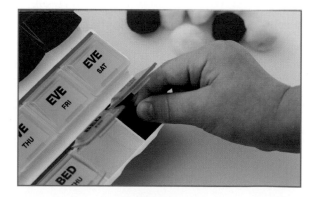

POM-POM NUMBER CATERPILLARS

It's time to count and make pom-pom caterpillars. How long will they be? Pick a Popsicle stick and we will see!

TARGET SKILLS: counting, one-to-one correspondence, number identification

MATERIALS

- 10–20 jumbo craft sticks, depending on the age of the child
- permanent marker
- 55–210 pom-poms, depending on the age of the child

DIRECTIONS TO MAKE

Write numbers 1 through 10 on the left edge of the jumbo craft sticks. If you have an older preschooler, write numbers 1 through 20 on the left edge of the jumbo craft sticks.

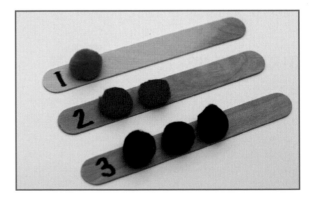

DIRECTIONS TO PLAY

1. The child will look at the number on the craft stick and identify the number.

2. Next, the child will count the number of pom-poms, placing them on the craft stick as they count.

3. If your child is older and doing the 1 through 20 craft sticks, the pom-poms will go past the edge of the craft sticks.

TIP: If you have a younger child, consider placing small stickers on the craft sticks to help your child count the correct number.

POPSICLE STICK NUMBER CLIP

With just a few stickers, we can create a counting activity. In this busy bag, children will practice counting and fine motor skills at the same time. They will count the stickers and clip the clothespins to the Popsicle sticks. This busy bag is quick and easy to put together.

TARGET SKILLS: counting, one-to-one correspondence, number identification, fine motor skills

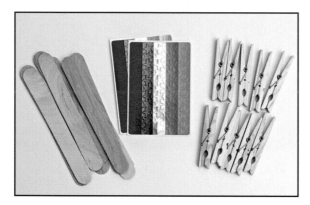

MATERIALS

- 10 jumbo craft sticks
- 55 small stickers
- 10 clothespins
- permanent marker

DIRECTIONS TO MAKE

1. Place stickers on the craft sticks, starting with one sticker on the first craft stick, then two stickers on another craft stick. Do this for numbers 1 through 10.

2. Write numbers 1 through 10 on both sides of the clothespins.

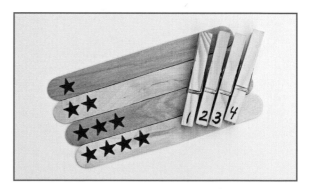

DIRECTIONS TO PLAY

1. Children will pick up a craft stick and count the number of stickers.

2. Then, they will clip the correct clothespin to the craft stick.

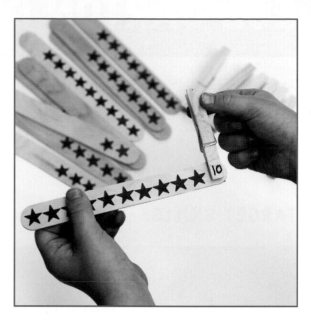

TIP: To make this self-checking, write the number on the back of the craft stick. Children will turn over the craft stick to match the two numbers and see if they counted correctly.

EGG CARTON COLOR MATCH

This busy bag is egg-cellent! Look no further than the recycling pile for this frugal busy bag. This bag is perfect for little ones still learning to match colors. As they match colors, they will be setting the stage for learning how to sort by color.

TARGET SKILLS: color matching, sorting by color

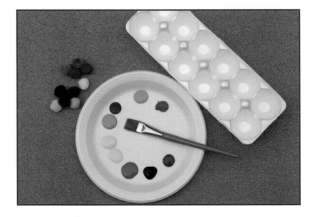

MATERIALS

- clean, empty egg carton
- paints, in various colors
- paintbrush
- scissors (optional)
- pom-poms that match the colors of the paints

DIRECTIONS TO MAKE

1. Paint each section of the egg carton with the various colors. It is fine to have more than one of each color.

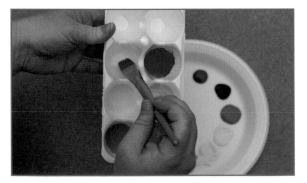

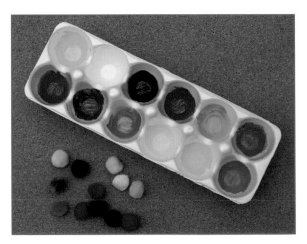

2. If you are placing this activity in a gallon size plastic storage bag, you will need to cut off the end of the egg carton so that there are only 10 sections.

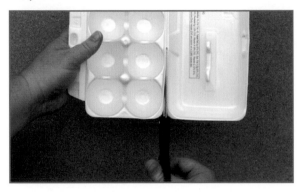

DIRECTIONS TO PLAY

Children will place the correct color pom-pom in each section of the painted egg carton, matching the colors as they play.

TIP: To help children work on their fine motor skills, have them use a clothespin to pick up the pom-poms and place them in the corresponding colored section.

SPOON NUMBER MATCH

Put those extra party supplies to good use! This quick and easy activity will allow you to use items you probably already have on hand. Don't let the simplicity fool you; this is a great activity to prepare your little learners for identifying numbers and counting.

TARGET SKILLS: number identification, counting

MATERIALS

- permanent marker
- 10 colored plastic spoons
- 10 clear plastic spoons

DIRECTIONS TO MAKE

1. Draw dots on the handles of the colored spoons. For example, make one dot on the first spoon, two dots on the second spoon, and so on. Do this for numbers 1 through 10.

2. Write numbers 1 through 10 on the heads of the clear spoons.

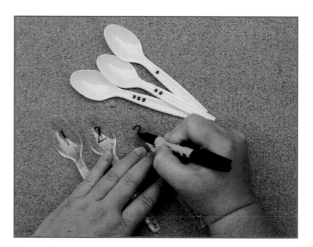

DIRECTIONS TO PLAY

Children will count the dots on the colored spoon handles. Then, children will find the matching number on a clear spoon and place it on top of the correct colored spoon.

COUNTING CATERPILLAR

What kid doesn't love bugs? Line the numbers up to create this creepy, crawly caterpillar. Kids will be working on placing numbers in order and making a fun number line.

TARGET SKILLS: numerical order, counting, number identification

MATERIALS

- disposable cup
- permanent marker
- 4 pieces of felt in various colors
- scissors
- squeezable paint with a writing tip

DIRECTIONS TO MAKE

1. Using the disposable cup and permanent marker, trace circles on the felt. If you are making this for a younger child, trace 11 circles. If you are making this for an older child, make 21 circles.

2. Cut out the felt circles.

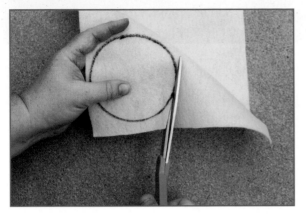

3. Using the writing tip on the squeezable paint, write the numbers 1 through 10 if you cut 11 circles, or numbers 1 through 20 if you cut 21 circles.

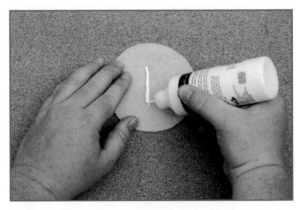

4. Paint a simple face on the extra circle.

5. Let the paint dry.

DIRECTIONS TO PLAY

Children will identify the numbers and place them in numerical order to make a number line caterpillar.

RAINBOW STICK

Head to the hardware store to prepare this activity. You'll make a rainbow stick ready to be clipped. Children will enjoy matching the colors and clipping the clothespins with this busy bag.

TARGET SKILLS: identifying and matching colors, fine motor skills

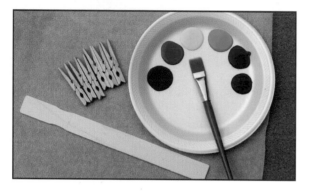

MATERIALS

- paint stirring stick
- acrylic paint in red, orange, yellow, green, blue, and purple
- small paint brush
- 6 clothespins
- plastic or disposable plate

DIRECTIONS TO MAKE

1. Protect your surface.

2. Paint the different colors on the paint stirring stick, leaving space between each color.

3. Paint a different color of paint on the end of each clothespin.

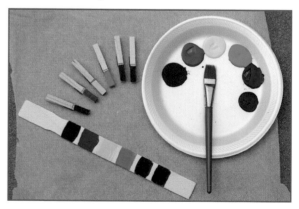

4. Let dry.

DIRECTIONS TO PLAY

Children will match up the colors and clip the clothespins to the paint stirring stick.

BLOCK SHADOWS

Using simple blocks, we can make a critical thinking activity for kids that will also work on spatial reasoning and math skills. Kids will love trying to guess how many blocks will fit into the outline.

TARGET SKILLS: visual discrimination, critical thinking, spatial reasoning

MATERIALS:

- 10 pieces of cardstock
- scissors
- 20 1-inch wooden blocks
- pencil
- marker
- laminator (optional)

DIRECTIONS TO MAKE

1. Cut the cardstock in half.

2. Place the wooden blocks onto the cardstock in a variety of different shapes with the edges of the blocks touching.

3. Using the pencil, trace around the block shape outline.

4. Using the marker, trace over the pencil line. Laminate the cards for durability, if you'd like.

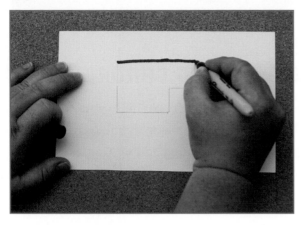

DIRECTIONS TO PLAY

Children will place the blocks into the outline. They will have to figure out how many blocks to use to fill the space.

TIP: Ask the child to guess how many blocks will fill each outline.

PART 2: LITERACY

EARLY LITERACY DEVELOPMENT IN YOUNG CHILDREN

Literacy and language are skills that go hand in hand, and they are so important to young learners. The toddler and preschool years are when these skills emerge and develop as children learn and explore language. From baby babbling to speaking, and then to reading and writing, language is something that unites us all.

Literacy, or the ability to read and write, is made up of many different things in the early years, including:

- Listening
- Speaking
- Reading
- Writing

Listening

As children listen to language, they are building vocabularies, learning how sounds work, and learning to communicate with others. Listening is an important skill for children learning to write because they need to hear the sounds as they write the letters on their paper. Plus, listening helps them learn to put sounds together when reading. Help develop listening skills in young children by reading lots of books to them, singing nursery rhymes, and talking to them about everything from a very early age. For example, when loading the washing machine with clothes, say, "First, we sort the clothes into darks and whites. Now, I'm putting in the dark clothes. Next, it's time for the soap. Finally, we're going to turn it on." While it may seem silly to describe everything you do, children will soak in all of the vocabulary and learn how speech works.

Speaking

What begins as babbling and gurgling sounds soon transforms into whole sentences. As children build their vocabularies and speaking skills, they develop communication skills. These skills later transfer to children's ability to express themselves through writing and reading aloud. Help develop these skills by letting children tell you about everything, asking them questions that require more than a yes or no answer, and encouraging them to sing nursery rhymes and children's songs with you.

Reading

Learning to read is one of the goals of many young children. They think they are "big" when they can read. When the two former skills, listening and speaking, are encouraged and explored throughout the early years, reading seems to be an easier skill to accomplish. Children who are ready to learn to read will often pretend to read familiar books and retell the story, start looking at beginning letters of words, and start trying to sound out words. Learning the alphabet and the sounds each letter makes is crucial to this time of literacy development. Encourage reading by talking about letter sounds and having children identify beginning sounds in words, starting with small three-letter words grouped in word families (like cat, bat, rat, sat, mat...) when teaching them to read.

Writing

Young children progress from scribbles, to letters, to words, and then to full sentences and paragraphs. The beginning stages of early writing are, well, messy. The scribbles on the page don't look like much at first, but children are making the connection from the spoken language to the written language. Encourage early writing development by allowing children to use various writing tools to make marks on paper, having them dictate to you what their drawings are while you write the words down, and giving them lots of fine motor development activities to help them build up their hand muscles to get ready to hold a pencil correctly.

The activities in this section have been developed to work on the reading and writing portion of early literacy. It's up to you to work on the listening and speaking portions. Mainly focusing on alphabet learning, this section will help your child on the road to literacy.

BUILD A WORD

Beginning readers start with sounding out small words first. This busy bag works on word families, or CVC words (consonant-vowel-consonant), and writing letters. Word families are words that share a common set of letters that make a similar sound. For example, the "_at" family words include cat, hat, bat, mat, rat, and sat. As children roll the dice and make words, they are beginning to read these CVC words. This activity is best suited for older preschoolers who are beginning to sound out words or kindergarten students at the same level.

TARGET SKILLS: letter sounds, CVC words, writing letters

MATERIALS

- three 1-inch wooden cubes
- green, red, and blue paint
- small paint brush
- plastic or disposable plate
- permanent marker
- white cardstock
- green, red, and blue markers
- laminator (optional)
- small dry erase board
- dry erase marker

DIRECTIONS TO MAKE

1. Paint each cube a separate color: green, red, and blue.

2. Write consonants on the sides of the green and red cubes and vowels on the blue cube.

Green Die	b, c, f, p, r, m
Red Die	t, d, g, p, m, n
Blue Die	a, e, i, o, u, a

3. Using half of a sheet of cardstock and the markers, trace three squares and outline them with colored markers in the following order: green, blue, red. Laminate for durability, if you'd like. This is a cue card for the child to place the cubes in the correct order.

DIRECTIONS TO PLAY

1. The child will roll the three dice, then place each cube on the cardstock with the squares ordered green, blue, then red.

2. They will say the sounds for each letter, then blend the sounds together to say the word.

3. Next, they will write the word on the dry erase board.

4. Now it's time to roll again! Repeat this over and over.

For an extra challenge: Have the kids sort the words they write into real and nonsense words.

NAME PUZZLES

Kids will love this busy bag that helps them identify names and faces of the people in their life, including themselves. Identifying names and learning the letters in their name is an important skill for children. Most children can identify their name before they can write it. This activity builds on that skill and helps children identify other important names in their life.

TARGET SKILLS: name identification, spelling names

MATERIALS
- cardstock
- scissors
- glue
- wallet-sized pictures of family members, including the child
- marker

DIRECTIONS TO MAKE

1. Cut the cardstock in half vertically, making the pieces measure 4 ¼ × 11 inches.

2. Turn the cardstock pieces so that you have a horizontal rectangle in front of you.

3. Glue the small pictures of family members, including the child, onto the left edge of the rectangle.

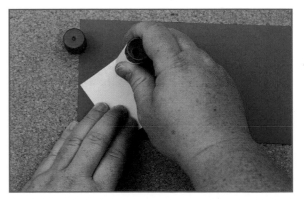

4. Using the marker, write name that corresponds with the family member's picture.

5. Cut the letters apart in zigzags, squiggles, slants, and the like so that each letter has a different and distinguishable shape.

DIRECTIONS FOR PLAY:

1. Mix up the puzzle pieces.

2. Have the child put the letter puzzles back together.

3. Have them identify the name using the picture as a reference.

TIP: To make this easier for young learners, make two identical name rectangles and leave one intact. Then, the child will use this one as a reference for matching the letters.

SPAGHETTI SPELLING

In this busy bag, children will form letters with yarn to practice building and distinguishing uppercase and lowercase letters. Later, when they learn to write, they will use this knowledge to help them form letters with a pencil.

TARGET SKILLS: forming uppercase and lowercase letters, letter identification

MATERIALS

- white yarn
- scissors
- 52 index cards
- marker
- laminator (optional)
- 1 piece of felt

DIRECTIONS TO MAKE

1. Cut the yarn into various lengths, from 2-inch pieces to 5-inch pieces.

2. Write the alphabet, both uppercase and lowercase letters, on the index cards for the children to use as a reference. Laminate for durability, if you'd like.

DIRECTIONS FOR PLAY

Have children use the yarn pieces to make letters, or even their name. They can place their yarn letters on the piece of felt so they won't move.

FISHING FOR LETTERS

There's a pond full of fish that need to be caught! Grab your fishing pole and cast your line to see what letter you will find. Children will go fishing for letters in this fun game to help them identify letters and work on hand-eye coordination. Challenge them to catch the fish in alphabetical order to see how well they can transfer their knowledge of the alphabet song to a slower pace.

TARGET SKILLS: identifying letters, hand-eye coordination, alphabetical order

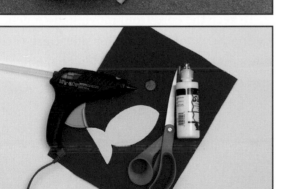

MATERIALS

- 18 pieces of felt in various colors
- scissors
- template (optional)
- squeezable paint with a writing tip
- hot glue gun
- 26 magnets
- ½-inch × 12-inch dowel rod
- drill
- 11/64-inch drill bit
- 9/64-inch venetian blind cord or other thin cord
- large washer

DIRECTIONS TO MAKE

1. Cut 52 identical fish shapes out of the felt. To make this easier, use the template on page 59 and trace it on to the felt before cutting.

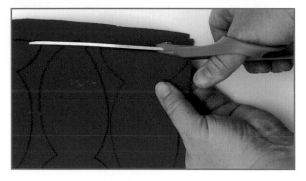

2. Using the paint, write the letters of the alphabet on 26 fish.

3. Hot glue one blank fish to a fish with a letter written on it, placing a magnet inside the mouth area before sealing completely.

4. Measure a ½ inch from the end of the dowel rod. Mark this spot with a pencil.

5. Drill a hole in the dowel rod at the place you marked.

6. Cut the cord to be 24 inches long.

7. Thread the cord through the hole and knot it. To keep the cord from moving too much, tie another knot on the other side, close to the dowel rod. There will be cord left hanging.

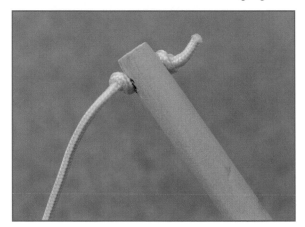

8. Tie the washer to the hanging end of the cord and double knot it.

DIRECTIONS TO PLAY

1. Spread the fish on the floor. Children will go fishing for letters.

2. When they catch a letter, they will say the letter name.

3. Then, they will go fishing for the next letter.

4. They will repeat this until they have caught all the letter fish.

For an extra challenge: Have your child start with A and work up to Z, placing the letters in alphabetical order on the floor.

TEMPLATE FOR FISH

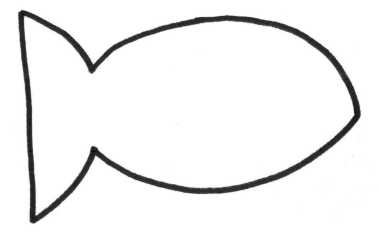

SPOON ABC MATCH

Who says spoons are just for eating? This busy bag takes ordinary household items and makes them into an alphabet game your kids will love to play. As children do this activity, they'll be learning to match uppercase and lowercase letters.

TARGET SKILLS: matching uppercase and lowercase letters, letter identification

MATERIALS

- 26 colored spoons
- 26 clear spoons
- permanent marker, or letter stickers with uppercase and lowercase letters

DIRECTIONS TO MAKE

1. Write one uppercase letter of the alphabet on each colored spoon. Or, if you are using alphabet stickers, place one uppercase letter of the alphabet on each colored spoon.

2. Write one lowercase letter of the alphabet on each clear spoon. Or, if you are using alphabet stickers, place one lowercase letter of the alphabet on each clear spoon.

DIRECTIONS TO PLAY

Children will match the uppercase and lower-case letter spoons, placing the clear spoon on top of the colored spoon.

TIP: For younger learners that still need help matching the uppercase and lowercase letters, write the letters (both uppercase and lowercase) on a sheet of cardstock paper for them to look at while completing this activity. Laminate for durability, if you'd like.

For an extra challenge: Have your child place the spoons in alphabetical order.

ABC STICKER PUZZLES

Children love puzzles. Let's make some puzzles to work on matching uppercase and lowercase letters. As they match the letters, they are practicing letter identification.

TARGET SKILLS: matching uppercase and lowercase letters, letter identification

MATERIALS

- 26 index cards
- large alphabet stickers, with both uppercase and lowercase letters
- scissors
- laminator (optional)

DIRECTIONS TO MAKE

1. Place an uppercase letter on the left side of the index card and the matching lowercase letter on the right side of the index card, leaving space between the letters.

2. Laminate for durability, if you'd like.

3. Cut the index cards in half. You can make zigzag lines, slants, curves, and the like for each one.

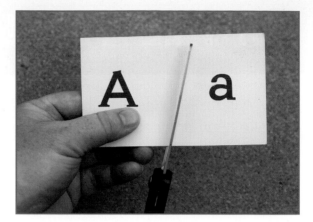

DIRECTIONS TO PLAY

Children will match the uppercase and lower-case letter puzzles.

TIP: If your child needs more support to match the uppercase and lowercase letters, write down the uppercase and lowercase letters on a piece of cardstock for them to use as a reference.

I SPY LETTERS!

"I spy with my little eye...the letter A!" Kids will search for letters in this easy-to-make I Spy bottle. Can they find them all? Only time will tell. This is a great activity to take in the car.

TARGET SKILL: letter identification

MATERIALS
- funnel
- rice
- dry, empty water bottle, preferably one without ridges and grooves
- letter beads, a through z
- hot glue gun
- marker
- cardstock
- laminator (optional)
- dry erase marker (optional)

DIRECTIONS TO MAKE

1. Using the funnel, place rice in the water bottle until it is most of the way full. As you are filling the water bottle with rice, place the letter beads in occasionally.

2. Hot glue the cap on the water bottle.

3. Shake it up to disperse the letter beads.

4. Write the letters of the alphabet on the cardstock. Laminate for durability, if you'd like.

DIRECTIONS TO PLAY

1. Children will roll the bottle around to search for the letters.

2. When they spy a letter, they can mark the letter off on their paper with either a pencil or a dry erase marker, if the page was laminated.

PART 3: FINE MOTOR SKILLS

DEVELOPING FINE MOTOR SKILLS

Motor skills are divided into two categories: *gross motor* and *fine motor*. Gross motor skills are the coordination of movements that are required for large movements, like crawling, running, jumping, throwing, and climbing. Fine motor skills are the coordination of movements that are required for small muscle movements, like using scissors, writing, opening water bottles, tying shoes, and buttoning shirts. Both sets of motor skills work together to help us function through our lives, but fine motor skills are the more detail-oriented of the two skills. Children start to use their hands right at birth to explore their own bodies and the world around them. Their fine motor skills develop as their bodies start to move and become more stable. They also learn to do more things with their hands as their cognitive, social, and emotional skills improve.

"Do you really need to focus on fine motor skills? Won't kids just pick up on them?"

To a certain extent, yes, kids will develop fine motor skills as they go through life, but I'd argue that they might not fully develop without some intentional practice. If we truly want to set up our children for success, I think it is important for us to set up opportunities for them to develop.

Developing fine motor skills doesn't have to be complicated, but it should always be fun! Some ideas for fun fine motor skills activities include:

- Playing with water guns and spray bottles to squirt water outside
- Using medicine droppers to transfer water from one bowl to another
- Tearing paper to make collages
- Playing with Play-Doh
- Using tongs to transfer pom-poms from one bowl to another
- Cutting Play-Doh "snakes" with scissors
- Playing with recycled bottles and jugs to practice twisting the tops on and off
- Coloring pictures

Children who haven't developed fine motor skills will have a harder time holding their pencils and writing legibly. They may color too hard or not hard enough. Others will have a hard time using scissors to cut paper. Developing fine motor skills is just as important for a growing child as learning to read and write.

So, how do you know if your child is on track for developing fine motor skills? Here is a list of developmental milestones to help you evaluate your child's fine motor skills.

Between the ages of 2 and 3 years, children should be able to:

- Stack five or more blocks
- Turn a doorknob
- Hold crayons or pencils, but not necessarily the way an adult would
- Draw a horizontal line
- Manipulate eating utensils, but not necessarily the way an adult would
- Remove shoes and socks
- Work puzzles with knobs

Between the ages of 3 and 4 years, children should be able to:

- Build a tower of nine or ten small blocks
- Use Play-Doh to make balls, snakes, cookies, and other simple shapes
- Build things with large linking blocks, such as Mega Bloks or Duplo
- Draw a circle without help
- Copy a cross (+)
- Copy drawing a square after an adult draws a square
- Start to hold a crayon or pencil with a mature grasp
- Cut across a piece of paper
- Manage buttons
- Put on most items of clothing by themselves, but may still need help with shirts and jackets
- Properly feed themselves with a spoon and fork
- Wash and dry hands
- String large beads
- Work puzzles with large pieces

Between the ages of 4 and 5 years, children should be able to:

- Start using one hand consistently for fine motor tasks
- Cut along a straight line with scissors
- Start cutting along a curved line, like a circle
- Draw a cross without help (+)
- Copy a square
- Begin to draw diagonal lines, like in a triangle
- Start to color inside the lines of a picture
- Start to draw recognizable pictures
- Build things with smaller linking blocks, such as Duplo or Lego
- Put on their own clothing, but may still need help with fasteners like buttons and zippers
- Start spreading butter or cut soft foods with a small table knife (with supervision)
- Start learning to print some capital letters

On the other side of the spectrum, if your child hasn't reached certain milestones by a certain age, it may be cause for concern. These red flags could signal that there may be an issue that needs to be addressed with a doctor or an occupational therapist. Below are some red flags to look for in your child.

Red flags for fine motor development (4 years)

- Movements seem shaky or stiff
- Arms and hands seem very weak
- Not able to cut across a piece of paper with scissors
- Cannot copy a cross (+)
- Not able to draw a circle and straight lines by themselves
- Cannot string ½-inch beads onto a string
- Cannot use a fork and spoon well
- Not able to put on their own pants, loose socks, and shoes

Red flags for fine motor development (5 years)

- Movements seem shaky or stiff
- Arms and hands seem very weak

- Not able to cut along a straight line
- Not holding crayons or pencils with thumb and fingers
- Not able to draw a circle, square, and cross (+)
- Not able to put on their own shirts, pants, socks, and shoes (with some help with fasteners)
- Not able to properly feed themselves with a spoon and fork

Two terms you will see in this section are bilateral coordination and hand-eye coordination. These two skills work together to help us use our hands in fine motor tasks.

Bilateral coordination is the use of both sides of the body to perform a task. Stabilizing a piece of paper with one hand while writing or cutting with the other hand are two examples. Almost all of the activities in this section involve using both hands to perform tasks.

Hand-eye coordination is the ability of the eyes to guide the hands in movements. We use hand-eye coordination in many things throughout our day: sports, handwriting, play, and life skills. Almost all of the activities in this section involve using the eyes to guide the hands in movements.

The activities in this section are all designed to develop fine motor skills in little hands. As children play with these busy bags, they will be strengthening their hand muscles, which will help them with many basic skills needed to function in everyday life.

BUTTON SNAKE

Sssssss! This Button Snake activity is not only cute, but it works on several skills at once. This activity targets buttoning skills, which is important when children are learning how to dress themselves.

TARGET SKILLS: fine motor skills, buttoning practice, hand-eye coordination, bilateral coordination

MATERIALS

- needle
- thread
- 2 large buttons
- 12-inch piece of ribbon
- 4 pieces of felt
- scissors

DIRECTIONS TO MAKE

1. Using the needle and thread, sew the large buttons to each end of the ribbon.

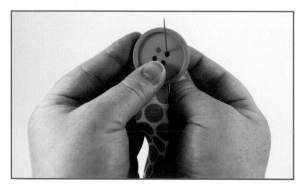

2. Cut the felt into 3 × 3-inch squares.

3. Fold the felt squares in half. At the crease, cut a slit that is large enough for the button to pass through.

DIRECTIONS TO PLAY

Have the child thread the button through the slits in the felt squares. They will repeat this until all the squares are on the ribbon. Then, they will have the task of taking the felt squares off the ribbon.

SILLY STRAW THREADING

Little fingers will take a wild ride in this crazy straw-threading activity. Children will practice threading the felt onto the silly straw for a silly fine motor experience.

TARGET SKILLS: fine motor skills, hand-eye coordination, bilateral coordination

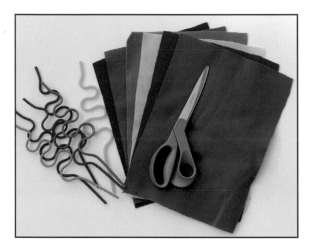

MATERIALS:

- 1 piece of felt per straw; match felt to each color of silly straw
- scissors
- 6 silly straws in various colors

DIRECTIONS TO MAKE

1. Cut 3 × 3-inch squares out of the felt.

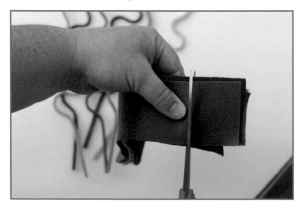

2. Fold the felt squares in half. At the crease, make a small snip in the center of the felt.

DIRECTIONS TO PLAY

Children will thread the felt squares from one end of the silly straw to the other, matching the colors as they play.

TIP: To make this a challenge for older children, use pony beads instead of felt squares to thread on the silly straws.

NUTS AND BOLTS

Look no further than the hardware store for this busy bag. Children will love to work with these tools to strengthen their little fingers. Twisting the nuts and bolts together is great practice for twisting other objects, like bottle caps.

TARGET SKILLS: fine motor skills, practicing twisting objects, bilateral coordination, hand-eye coordination

MATERIALS

- 10 large nuts
- 10 large bolts

DIRECTIONS TO MAKE

Gather your materials. This one is so simple there isn't anything to make!

DIRECTIONS TO PLAY

Children will twist the nuts and bolts together.

TIP: To add another learning twist to this activity, very lightly spray paint each nut and bolt pair with a different color of paint to make this a color matching activity as well as a fine motor activity. Make sure to spray paint the nuts and bolts very lightly to keep the threads from getting stuck.

SHOE TYING PRACTICE BOARD

Tying shoes is one of those skills that seems to give kids a lot of trouble. Once they master this skill, they will smile from ear to ear. This busy bag will help them practice tying their shoes and work on fine motor skills, too.

TARGET SKILLS: fine motor skills, self-dressing skills, bilateral coordination, hand-eye coordination

MATERIALS

- wooden plaque (6 inches × 9 inches)
- tape measure
- pencil
- ¼-inch drill bit
- drill
- sand paper
- acrylic paint
- 45-inch shoelace

DIRECTIONS TO MAKE

1. Orient the wooden plaque vertically. Using a tape measure, find the halfway point across the board horizontally. Then, find the halfway point across the board vertically. Mark this spot with a pencil. This will be your midpoint.

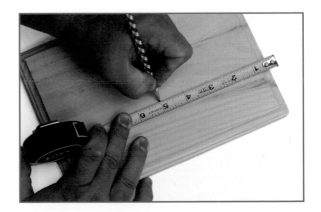

2. From the midpoint, measure ¾ inch out on each side, horizontally. These will be your reference lines to drill holes.

3. From your outside reference point, place a ruler vertically along the board. Mark three additional holes at 1-inch intervals: two above and one below the marking. Repeat on the other side.

4. Drill holes where you made your marks on the wooden plaque. Make pairs of holes to look like a shoe.

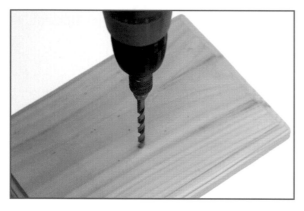

5. Sand over the holes to eliminate snags or splinters.

DIRECTIONS TO PLAY

Children will practice tying their shoes.

6. Paint the plaque.

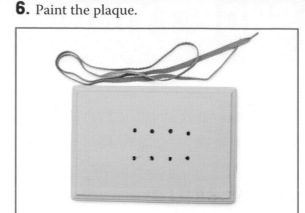

7. Lace up the board with the shoelace, leaving the ends free for the children to practice tying shoelaces.

ZIPPER BOARD

Zip! Zip! Zip! Kids will practice using zippers with this zipper board activity. While they're playing, they'll be practicing skills for dressing themselves, which they'll use for the rest of their lives. Younger children will love to zip the zippers back and forth.

TARGET SKILLS: fine motor skills, self-dressing skills

MATERIALS

- hot glue gun
- 1 piece of felt
- cardboard from a box
- utility knife
- 7-inch or 9-inch zippers

DIRECTIONS TO MAKE

1. Hot glue the felt to the cardboard.

2. Trim the cardboard around the felt with a utility knife.

3. Very carefully, hot glue both sides of the zippers to the felt board. Make sure not to get the hot glue on the zipper teeth.

4. Allow to cool.

DIRECTIONS TO PLAY

Children will practice zipping the zippers open and closed.

LACING SHAPES

Up, down, up, down, all the way around the shape! Children will practice lacing in this busy bag. Lacing is the childhood equivalent to sewing, and it takes lots of coordination to use both hands at once.

TARGET SKILLS: fine motor skills, lacing, bilateral coordination, hand-eye coordination

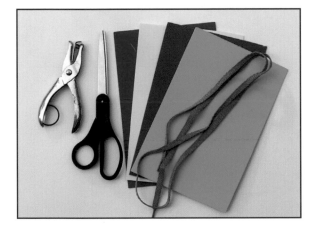

MATERIALS

- craft foam sheets
- scissors
- single hole punch
- shoe laces

DIRECTIONS TO MAKE

1. Cut shapes such as a circle, triangle, square, and diamond out of the craft foam sheets.

2. Using the single hole punch, poke holes around the shapes.

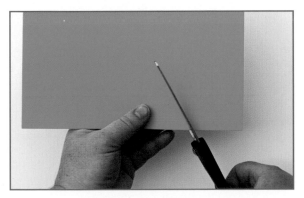

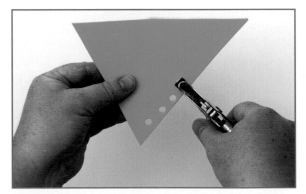

DIRECTIONS TO PLAY

Children will use the shoelaces to thread
through the holes in the shapes.

PIPE CLEANER POKE

Make a silly sculpture out of pipe cleaners in this busy bag. Is it a lion with an untamed mane or an alien with lots of arms? This busy bag is sure to make them giggle. This is perfect for younger preschoolers.

TARGET SKILLS: fine motor skills, lacing, hand-eye coordination, bilateral coordination

MATERIALS

- 15 pipe cleaners
- whiffle ball, or plastic practice golf balls with holes

DIRECTIONS TO MAKE

Gather materials. There's nothing to make with this one!

DIRECTIONS TO PLAY

Children will use the pipe cleaners to poke through the holes in the ball.

PUT IT IN YOUR WALLET

Children love to play with wallets and wonder what's inside. Little hands that accidentally find their mommy's purse will often take credit cards out of the wallet. Let's harness that natural curiosity with this simple activity. Young children will love to play this over and over.

TARGET SKILLS: fine motor skills, pincer grasp, bilateral coordination, hand-eye coordination

MATERIALS

- credit card
- thin cardboard from a cereal box
- scissors
- colored markers
- wallet with lots of credit card compartments
- wallet-size pictures of family members (optional)
- laminator (optional)

DIRECTIONS TO MAKE

1. Trace the credit card on the thin cardboard from a cereal box. Trace as many pieces as you need to fill up the wallet credit card compartments.

2. Cut out the thin cardboard.

3. Decorate the pieces of cardboard with different patterns, like stars, hearts, squiggles, and circles.

4. Place the cardboard pieces inside the credit card compartments of the wallet.

5. If you are using wallet-size pictures of family members, you may want to laminate the pictures to make them sturdier.

DIRECTIONS TO PLAY

Children will take the cardboard pieces out of the wallet and then put them back in.

TIP: If you have any old hotel key cards, place these in the wallet, too. Children love to pretend they have credit cards.

PHOTO BOOK TRACING

Let little hands practice tracing lines and begin to write letters in this activity. With the help of a highlighted line, children will trace letters. This is a great on-the-go activity.

TARGET SKILLS: fine motor skills, tracing letters, writing, hand-eye coordination, bilateral coordination

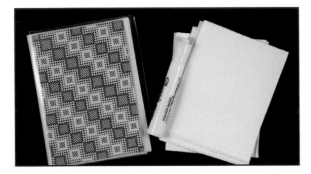

MATERIALS

- 13 pieces of paper
- scissors
- 4 × 6-inch photo book
- highlighter
- dry erase marker

DIRECTIONS TO MAKE

1. Fold the paper in half vertically and horizontally. Cut on these lines. Trim the paper so it fits into the 4 × 6-inch photo book.

2. Using the highlighter, write the alphabet (both uppercase and lowercase letters) on the paper pieces. You could draw shapes, too.

3. Place the paper pieces into the photo book.

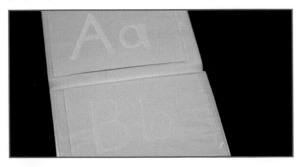

DIRECTIONS TO PLAY

Children will use the dry erase marker to trace the letters on each page.

BUTTON TURKEY

Practice buttoning skills with this adorable little turkey. As children manipulate the buttons, they are strengthening their self-dressing skills, as well as building their hand muscles.

TARGET SKILLS: fine motor skills, buttoning skills, self-dressing skills, hand-eye coordination, bilateral coordination

MATERIALS

- 1 piece of brown felt
- 1 piece of tan felt
- 1 piece of red felt
- 1 piece of orange felt
- 1 piece of green felt
- scissors
- buttons
- needle
- thread
- permanent marker
- hot glue
- permanent marker

DIRECTIONS TO MAKE

1. Trace an 8-inch circle on the brown felt. Cut out the circle.

2. Using the tan felt, make the turkey head in the shape of a peanut about 5 inches long. Hot glue it to the bottom center of the circle.

3. Using the red felt, cut the turkey's snood. Hot glue it to the turkey head.

4. Cut a small triangle beak. Hot glue it to the turkey head, overlapping the red snood.

5. Draw in the eyes with a permanent marker.

6. Sew buttons around the edge on the top half of the circle.

7. Draw feather shapes about 7 inches long on the red, orange, and green felt. Make the top pointed and the bottom straight.

8. Cut out the feathers.

9. Fold the bottom edge of the feathers to make a crease. Cut a small slit in the crease to make a hole for the buttons to go through.

DIRECTIONS TO PLAY

Children will place the feathers on the buttons. When they have buttoned all the feathers on, it will look like a turkey.

BUTTON FLOWERS

In this activity, children will make a bouquet of flowers that will live forever. Little hands will practice buttoning skills, dexterity, and bilateral coordination through this busy bag.

TARGET SKILLS: fine motor skills, buttoning skills, self-dressing skills, hand-eye coordination, bilateral coordination

MATERIALS

- pipe cleaners
- large buttons
- felt
- template (optional)
- scissors

DIRECTIONS TO MAKE

1. Poke both ends of the pipe cleaner through two of the buttonholes. Pull the pipe cleaner all the way through so that both ends of the pipe cleaner are even.

2. Twist the ends of the pipe cleaner together. This is going to be the stem of the flower.

3. Take the felt and cut large flower shapes about 3½ to 4 inches in diameter. I like to use a template (as shown below) to keep the flowers more consistent.

4. Cut a slit in the middle of the flower pieces large enough for the button to pass through the hole.

DIRECTIONS TO PLAY

Children will place the flower shapes onto the button, making a flower on a stem when finished.

POKER CHIP PUSH

Put away the cards and bring out the poker chips with this activity. As they strengthen their hand muscles, little ones will love to hear the clink of the chips falling into the coffee can. This activity works on the pincer grasp, when children hold items with their thumb and index finger.

TARGET SKILLS: fine motor skills, pincer grasp, hand-eye coordination

MATERIALS

- utility knife
- recycled coffee can with a lid
- poker chips
- contact paper or spray paint (optional)

DIRECTIONS TO MAKE

1. Using the utility knife, cut a rectangular slit large enough for poker chips to go through on the lid of the coffee can.

2. Cover the coffee can with contact paper or spray paint, if you would like.

DIRECTIONS TO PLAY

Children will poke the poker chips into the slit of the lid of the coffee can.

TIP: To make this an educational activity, write letters and numbers on the poker chips. Have the child place the poker chips with letters or numbers in the coffee can in alphabetical or numerical order.

FELT BUTTON CHAIN

As a child, I loved to make paper chains. In this busy bag, we'll trade in the paper for felt and use the chain for a fine motor skill activity.

TARGET SKILLS: fine motor skills, buttoning skills, hand-eye coordination, bilateral coordination

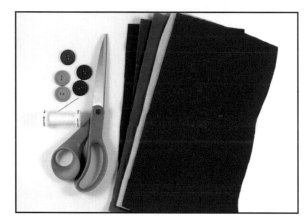

MATERIALS

- 3 pieces of felt
- scissors
- buttons
- thread
- needle

DIRECTIONS TO MAKE

1. Orient the felt vertically, then cut the felt into strips 2½ inches wide.

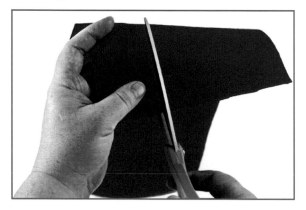

2. Fold one edge of each felt strip about 1 inch from the end. On the crease, cut a slit large enough for the button to pass through.

3. Sew a button on the other end of the felt strip.

DIRECTIONS TO PLAY

1. Children will button the first strip together.

2. They will place the second felt strip into the loop of the first felt chain and button it.

3. Play continues until the child has made a chain out of the felt strips.

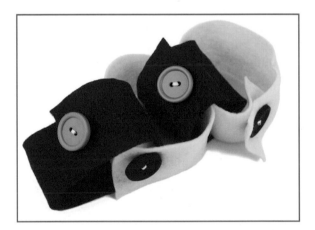

PART 4: JUST FOR FUN

PLAY IN THE EARLY YEARS

There's no doubt about it: kids love to have fun! Whether they're in a water balloon fight or romping around on the playground, kids are natural fun-seekers. As adults, we too often forget to have fun, and sometimes we forget that childhood is supposed to be fun, too. Kids learn through play, so even if they look like they are "just playing," they are learning, too.

Like crying or making sounds, children don't have to be taught to play. Play is innate, and is essentially a child's "work." It helps children's brains grow while also being a lot of fun. Play helps children:

- build confidence
- feel loved, happy, and safe
- develop social skills, language, and communication
- learn about caring for others and the environment
- develop physical skills
- connect and refine pathways in their brain

There are many types of play, and all of them are important to children.

Unoccupied Play: For the first three months of life, babies partake in unoccupied play. This type of play involves movements with no clear purpose, but it has been identified as an initial and important early stage of play.

Solitary Play: Three-month-old to 18-month-old babies will spend much of their time playing on their own. During solitary play, children may not even notice other children sitting nearby as they are too busy exploring their worlds and watching, grabbing, and rattling objects.

Onlooker Play: Onlooker play, which is where children watch other children play, usually occurs during the toddler years. At this stage, children learn how to relate to others and learn language. Although children may ask questions of other children, there is rarely an effort to join them in play.

Parallel Play: From the age of 18 months up to age two, children begin to play alongside other children, but without interaction. This type of play helps them understand the idea of property rights, such as the concept of "mine."

Associative Play: Around the age of three, children become more interested in other children than their toys. Associative play helps them learn the dos and don'ts of getting along with others.

Social Play: Children around the age of four begin to socialize more with other children. By interacting with other children during play settings, your child learns social rules such as give, take, and cooperate.

Physical Play: Physical play offers a chance for children to exercise and develop muscle strength. Simple activities such as running, jumping, and playing games such as hide-and-seek and tag are really important.

Constructive Play: Constructive play starts in infancy and becomes more complex as a child grows. When children manipulate their environment to create things, they are engaged in constructive play. In constructive play, children experiment with materials, build towers with blocks, construct objects with miscellaneous loose parts, play in the sand, and draw sidewalk murals with chalk.

Expressive Play: Expressive play allows children to be in complete control of their actions and experiences, which boosts their confidence. Beanbags, rhythm instruments, and dress-up clothes are great tools to promote expressive play.

Play does not need to involve expensive or elaborate toys. In fact, these items often hinder creativity and create limits to play. Children need toys and materials to play with that are open-ended in nature. This is why many children are more interested in the box a toy came in than the toy itself! One of the keys to supporting your child's play effectively is to avoid taking over. The best approach is to allow them to direct the play on their own.

While the bulk of the activities in this book are learning based, this section is just for fun. It will foster playful experiences for your child.

TIP: Several of the activities in this chapter are made with felt. Don't throw away the scraps! You can save your felt scraps to use for other projects in the book.

MATCHING GAME

Matching games are a childhood staple. This matching game is simple to make and will enhance memory skills in children.

TARGET SKILLS: visual discrimination, matching similar objects, memory skills

MATERIALS

- 20 1½-inch wooden disks
- pencil
- 10 pieces of patterned scrapbook paper
- scissors
- Mod Podge
- craft brush

DIRECTIONS TO MAKE

1. Trace the wooden disks onto the scrapbook paper. You will need to trace two circles on each page.

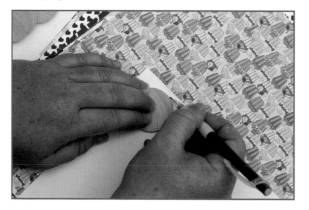

2. Cut the circles, trimming them to be smaller than the wooden disks.

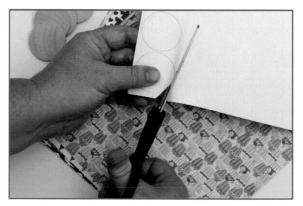

3. Using the Mod Podge, glue each paper circle to the wooden disks. Then, Mod Podge over the paper circles to seal them.

4. Let dry.

DIRECTIONS TO PLAY

1. Children will place all of the wooden disks paper-side down.

2. They will pick two wooden disks. If they are a match, they get to keep the match. If they aren't a match, they must turn the disks back over.

3. Play continues until all the matches have been found.

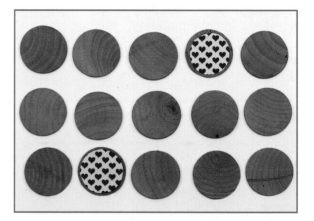

SOCK FISHING GAME

Kids will love to go fishing for these adorable fish made from socks. Young children are fascinated with magnets and how they work, so your child's curiosity will be piqued. These initial interactions with magnets and metal washers are the foundation for science exploration later in life.

TARGET SKILLS: hand-eye coordination, science exploration

MATERIALS

- ½-inch × 12-inch dowel rod
- ruler
- pencil
- scissors
- drill
- ¹¹⁄₆₄-inch drill bit
- ⁹⁄₆₄-inch venetian blind cord or other thin cord
- metal washer
- 6 magnets
- 6 colorful socks
- fiberfill
- yarn
- small buttons for eyes (optional)

DIRECTIONS TO MAKE

1. Measure a ½ inch from the end of the dowel rod. Mark this spot with a pencil.

2. Drill a hole in the dowel rod at the place you marked.

3. Cut the cord to 24 inches long.

4. Thread the cord through the hole and knot it. To keep the cord from moving too much, tie another knot on the other side close to the dowel rod. There will be cord left hanging.

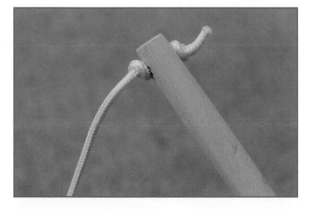

5. Tie the washer to the end of the hanging cord and double knot it.

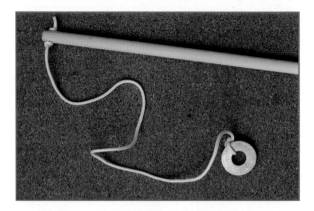

6. Place a magnet in the toe of each sock. Place a handful of fiberfill inside the sock until about half of the sock is full.

7. Wrap the yarn around the sock several times to cinch it closed. Double knot the yarn. Cut the extra yarn away.

8. Cut the rest of the sock into a tail fin shape.

9. Sew buttons on for eyes, if you'd like.

DIRECTIONS TO PLAY

Have the child hold the fishing pole and try to catch a fish with the metal washer.

COOKIE CUTTER MATCH-UP

Get a little help from the kitchen for this busy bag. Using ordinary cookie cutters, this activity will work on visual discrimination and matching objects. This is perfect for younger children.

TARGET SKILLS: visual discrimination, matching objects

MATERIALS

- 16 cookie cutters
- 4 pieces of cardstock
- pencil
- marker
- laminator (optional)

DIRECTIONS TO MAKE

1. Arrange the cookie cutters on the cardstock. You should be able to fit about four to a page.

2. Trace around the cookie cutters with the pencil.

3. Trace over the pencil lines with the marker.

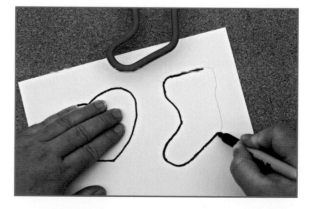

4. Laminate the cardstock pieces for durability, if you'd like.

DIRECTIONS TO PLAY

Children will match the cookie cutters to the correct outline.

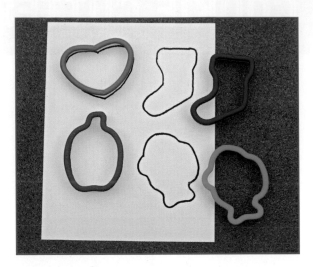

BUILD A FACE

Kids will love making up different combinations of silly faces in this busy bag. The possibilities are endless!

TARGET SKILLS: fun, pretending

MATERIALS

- 1 piece of skin-toned felt
- 1 piece of brown felt
- 1 piece of yellow felt
- 1 piece of bright pink felt
- 1 piece of red felt
- 1 piece of dark red felt
- scissors

DIRECTIONS TO MAKE

1. Using the skin-toned felt, cut out a face (don't forget to account for the ears!). Also cut out a nose.

2. Using the rest of the felt, cut various body and hair pieces. If you want, you can make several sets out of various felt colors.

DIRECTIONS TO PLAY

Children will use the felt pieces to build a face. They can mix and match the pieces to make different combinations.

BUILD AN OCEAN

Ah, the ocean. The perfect place for an under-the-sea adventure. Children will get to make up their very own ocean scene and pretend they are swimming with the fish in this activity.

TARGET SKILLS: fun, pretending

MATERIALS

- hot glue gun
- 1 piece of blue felt
- cardboard from a box
- utility knife
- pieces of felt in various colors
- scissors
- googly eyes

DIRECTIONS TO MAKE

1. Hot glue the blue felt to the cardboard.

2. Trim the cardboard around the edge of the blue felt with the utility knife.

3. Cut various ocean shapes, including fish, out of the colored felt.

4. Glue the googly eyes to the fish.

DIRECTIONS TO PLAY

Children will build an ocean scene and
pretend with the felt pieces.

BUILD A MONSTER

Let imaginations run wild as children build their very own monsters. How many eyes does he have? Or what about his horns? These monsters can be as silly as children want to make them.

TARGET SKILLS: fun, pretending

MATERIALS

- 1 piece of neon green felt
- 1 piece of green felt
- 1 piece of red felt
- 1 piece of yellow felt
- 1 piece of orange felt
- 1 piece of black felt
- scissors
- 8 large googly eyes

DIRECTIONS TO MAKE

1. Cut the felt shapes for the monster. In my monster, I cut out horns, eyes, a nose, and a mouth. If you want, you can make several sets out of various felt colors.

DIRECTIONS TO PLAY

Children will use the various pieces to build
a monster. They can use their imagination to
make the craziest monsters ever.

BUILD A ROBOT

Wouldn't it be great if we had a robot around to tackle some of our household tasks? Let children create their very own robot with this fun busy bag. They will love pretending they have a robot. Don't forget to have them name it and tell you what the robot does.

TARGET SKILLS: fun, pretending

MATERIALS

- 1 piece of gray felt
- pieces of felt in various colors
- scissors

DIRECTIONS TO MAKE

1. Cut a large gray rectangle and a smaller one for the body and head. My robot's body was about 4 × 6 inches and the head was 2½ × 3 inches. Cut out two T-shaped legs. You can also make paper versions of the shapes to use as templates.

2. Using felt of various colors, create the robot's hands, eyes, mouth, and buttons.

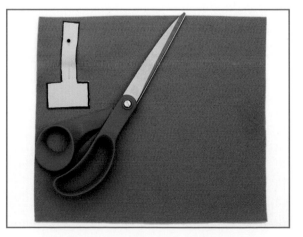

DIRECTIONS TO PLAY

Children will use the various pieces to build a robot.

BUILD A JACK-O-LANTERN

There is magic in the night when pumpkins glow by moonlight. Let your little one decorate their own pumpkin without all the gooey mess of carving a real pumpkin. They can mix and match the shapes to make each one different.

TARGET SKILLS: fun, pretending

MATERIALS

- 1 piece of orange felt
- 1 piece of black felt
- template (optional)
- scissors

DIRECTIONS TO MAKE

1. Using the orange felt, cut out a large pumpkin shape.

2. Using the template on page 112, cut the black felt to make the jack-o-lantern's eyes, nose, and mouth.

DIRECTIONS FOR PLAY

Children will use the felt pieces to mix, match, and make a jack-o-lantern.

BUILD A GINGERBREAD MAN

"Run, run, as fast as you can. You can't catch me, I'm the gingerbread man!" Children will decorate their very own gingerbread cookie that they won't have to chase down. This playful activity could be used during the winter holidays.

TARGET SKILLS: fun, pretending

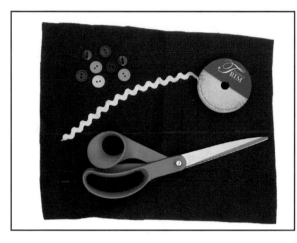

MATERIALS

- 1 piece of brown felt
- template (optional)
- scissors
- small white ric-rac trim
- 8 small buttons approximately ½ inch in diameter

DIRECTIONS TO MAKE

1. Using the template on page 114, cut a gingerbread man shape out of the brown felt.

2. Cut the small white ric-rac trim into six 2-inch pieces and two 3-inch pieces.

DIRECTIONS TO PLAY

Children will decorate a gingerbread man.

BUILD A SNOWMAN

Stay in from the cold and dress up the snowman from the warmth of your own home with this busy bag. No mittens required.

TARGET SKILLS: fun, pretending

MATERIALS

- 1 piece of white felt
- 1 piece of black felt
- 1 piece of red felt
- 1 piece of orange felt
- 1 piece of brown felt
- 1 piece of yellow felt
- template (optional)
- scissors
- 5 small black buttons

DIRECTIONS TO MAKE

1. Using the white felt, cut out a snowman shape about 11 inches tall.

2. Use the templates on page 116 and cut out the snowman's details from the various colored felts.

DIRECTIONS TO PLAY

Children will make a snowman out of the felt pieces and buttons.

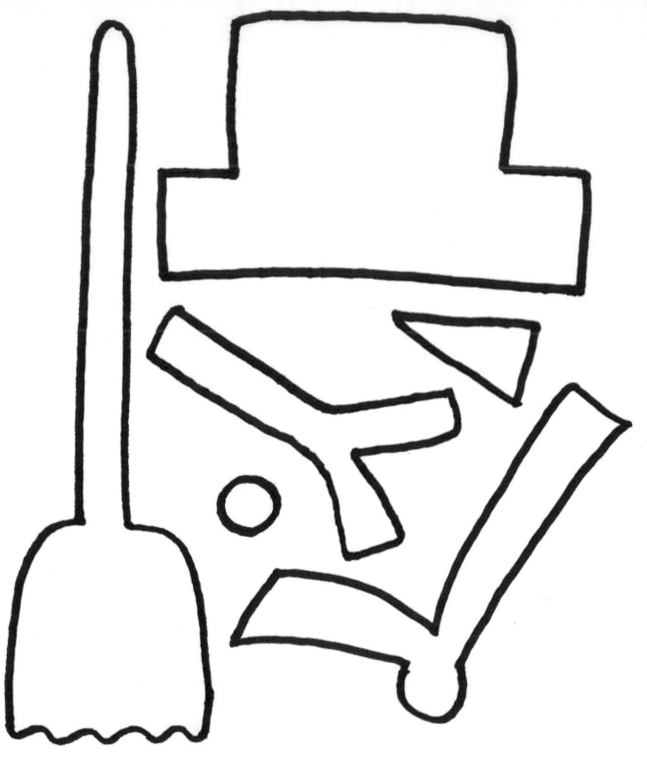

PEG DOLL DRESS UP

Everyone loves a good game of dress-up. With this upgraded version of paper dolls, children will have fun mixing and matching clothing to dress the doll.

TARGET SKILLS: fun, pretending

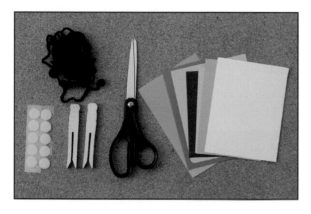

MATERIALS

- brown, black, or yellow yarn
- hot glue
- 2 flat clothespins
- various patterned cardstock, or colored cardstock that is decorated with markers
- template (optional)
- permanent marker
- laminator (optional)
- 4 Velcro dots

DIRECTIONS TO MAKE

1. Cut small pieces of yarn to make hair for the clothespin dolls. Hot glue these on the flat clothespins.

2. Using the patterned cardstock and the templates on page 118, cut various clothing shapes. Laminate these pieces for durability, if you'd like.

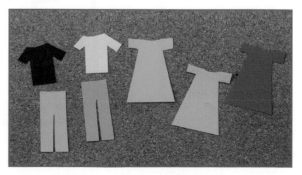

3. With a permanent marker, draw eyes, a nose, and a mouth on the clothespin.

4. Place two Velcro dots on each clothespin doll. Place the other side of the Velcro dots on the back of the clothing pieces.

DIRECTIONS TO PLAY

Children will place the clothing pieces on the dolls. They can mix and match the clothing as they play.

TEMPLATE FOR CLOTHES

JEWELRY BOX MATCH-UP

Here's a new twist on the matching game that little ones will love. Find the box and its matching top to win this game. Young toddlers will enjoy opening and closing the boxes, while preschoolers will enjoy playing a matching game.

TARGET SKILLS: visual discrimination, matching similar objects, fine motor skills

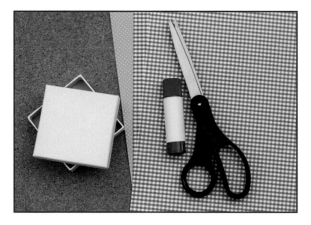

MATERIALS

- 10 small cardboard jewelry boxes
- 10 pieces of patterned scrapbook paper
- glue
- scissors

DIRECTIONS TO MAKE

1. Trace the boxes two times on the patterned paper. You will want to have two pieces that are the same for each box.

2. Cut out the paper pieces. Trim them so the pieces fit inside the top and bottom of the box.

3. Glue the paper pieces on the inside of the boxes. There should be a matching top piece and a bottom piece for each box.

DIRECTIONS TO PLAY

1. Pull the boxes apart and mix them up, patterned side down.

2. Children will pick up two boxes and see if they match. If they do, they will put them together. If they don't match, the boxes are placed faced down again.

3. Repeat until all of the boxes and lids are matched up.

TIP: To make this a color matching activity, use construction paper in every shade of the rainbow.

TIP: The jewelry boxes for this activity were found in the jewelry-making section of the local craft store.

POPSICLE STICK PICTURE PUZZLES

Who wouldn't love a puzzle with their very own face on it? Children will love these picture puzzles, especially when they see familiar faces staring back at them.

TARGET SKILLS: logical thinking

MATERIALS

- 4 × 6-inch pictures of familiar faces printed on regular computer paper
- scissors
- 8 jumbo craft sticks for each picture
- painter's tape
- Mod Podge
- craft brush
- utility knife

DIRECTIONS TO MAKE

1. Trim the excess paper from the printed photo with scissors. Using the trimmed photo as a guide, place the jumbo craft sticks side by side so they are touching. You will need 8 for each 4 × 6-inch picture.

2. Using the painter's tape, tape the craft sticks together. Turn the connected sticks over so the tape is on the bottom.

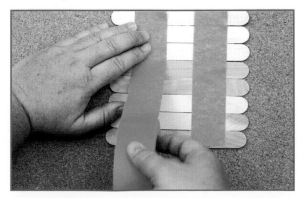

3. Glue the picture on the top side of the craft sticks using the Mod Podge.

4. Cover the top of the picture with Mod Podge to seal. Allow to dry.

5. When dry, remove the painter's tape.

6. Use the utility knife to cut the craft sticks and picture apart.

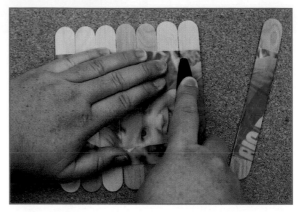

DIRECTIONS TO PLAY

1. Children will place the craft sticks in order. When they are finished, they will see a picture.

2. This is a self-checking activity because if the child sees the picture does not look correct, they will need to rearrange the craft sticks to complete the picture puzzle correctly.

POPSICLE STICK HIGHWAY

Zoom! Crash! Bump! Smash! Give a child a toy car and they will play for hours. This simple busy bag is perfect for the car lover in your life.

TARGET SKILLS: pretending

MATERIALS

- 20 jumbo craft sticks
- black paint
- craft brush
- yellow paint pen
- small toy car

DIRECTIONS TO MAKE

1. Protect your surface. Paint the craft sticks with black paint on one side. Let dry.

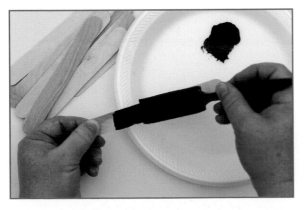

2. Using the yellow paint pen, mark small lines in the middle of the craft stick to resemble the lines on a road.

DIRECTIONS TO PLAY

1. Children will build their road using the craft sticks.

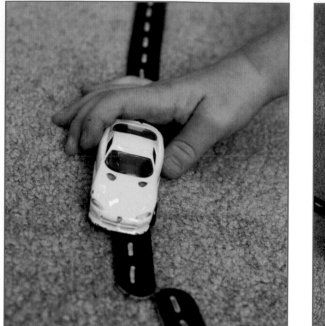

2. Using a small toy car, they can pretend they are driving along the road.

TIP: To add a little math to this activity, have your child make different shapes with the road sticks.

RICE SENSORY BIN

This colorful sensory experience is sure to please little hands. Playing with the rice is calming and fun for children. Sensory play is a staple of childhood learning and experiences.

TARGET SKILLS: sensory play, fun

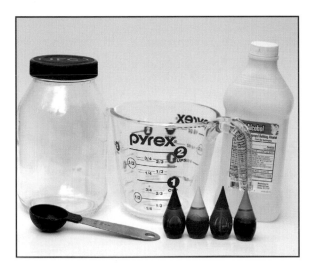

MATERIALS

- large baking sheets
- aluminum foil, parchment paper, or wax paper
- tablespoon
- rubbing alcohol
- 1-quart jar
- 1 (10-pound) bag of rice
- 2-cup measuring cup
- food coloring
- 15-quart shallow plastic box with a lid
- small items for play: spoons, toy bulldozers, funnels, measuring cups, etc.

DIRECTIONS TO MAKE

1. Line baking sheets with aluminum foil, parchment paper, or wax paper.

2. Preheat oven to 175°F.

3. Pour 1 tablespoon of rubbing alcohol in the bottom of a 1-quart jar.

4. Pour 20 drops of food coloring into the jar, and then pour 2 cups of uncooked rice in the jar.

5. Place the lid on the jar and shake it until the rice is evenly colored.

6. Pour onto the lined baking sheet. Spread it into an even layer. This will cover about half of the baking sheet.

7. Repeat steps 3 through 6 with the same color. When done, pour rice on the other half of the baking sheet and spread into an even layer.

8. Place in oven for 15 minutes. When the time is done, check to see if the rice is dry. If it is, pour it into the 15-quart shallow plastic box with lid. If the rice isn't dry, place the baking sheet back in the oven for 5 to 10 more minutes.

9. Repeat steps 1 through 8 with the other colors until the bag of rice is gone.

DIRECTIONS FOR PLAY

1. Place spoons, toy bulldozers, funnels, measuring cups, and other small items into the bin on top of the rice.

2. Children will play with the rice. They'll love this sensory experience. Children will scoop, pour, and funnel the rice for quite some time.

3. When the child is finished playing with the rice, place the lid on top and store until another playtime.

For an extra challenge: Hide pieces to an alphabet puzzle in the rice. As they find the hidden letters, have your child complete the puzzle.

TIP: To keep the rice mess to a minimum, spread a round tablecloth under the bin and the child. When they are finished playing, pour the rice that has been spilled into the storage bin. Or, have them play this on the back porch where clean-up is easy.

ACKNOWLEDGMENTS

For Ray—thank you for supporting me in this endeavor. You were my rock when I needed it and my biggest cheerleader. Thank you for believing in me when I didn't believe in myself. I'm forever grateful for your help with taking the photos for this book while I was a hand model.

For Jonah and Asher—you are my everything. I'm thankful God chose me to be your mommy.

For all of my fellow kids activities bloggers—you inspire me daily. Thank you for challenging me to think of new ways to make learning fun.

ABOUT THE AUTHOR

SARA McCLURE is a mom and certified teacher with experience in early childhood education. She holds a bachelor's degree in Child and Family Studies with an emphasis on Early Childhood Education for pre-K through fourth grade, and a master's degree in Urban Education. After five years of classroom teaching, she transitioned to homeschooling her two boys. To save her sanity, she uses busy bags to keep her younger son entertained while she teaches the older son. She is the blogger at HappyBrownHouse.com where she shares recipes, meaningful learning activities for kids, and a peek into her homeschooling life.